A Walk on the
Great Barrier Reef

A Walk on the Great Barrier Reef

by Caroline Arnold/photographs by Arthur Arnold

With additional photographs by Marty Snyderman,
Alex Kerstitch, Jeff Rotman, and Stan Keiser

A Carolrhoda Nature Watch Book

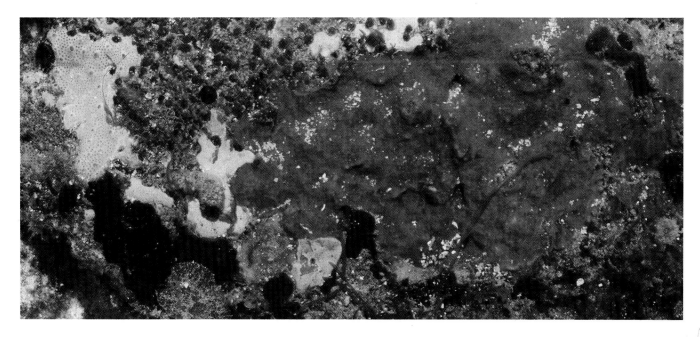

 Carolrhoda Books, Inc./Minneapolis

*Thanks to Dr. Franklin Barnwell, Professor
and Head of the Department of Ecology
and Behavioral Biology, University of Minnesota,
for his assistance with this book*

The author and photographer wish to thank Libby and
Bob Scott for their assistance with this project.

Text copyright © 1988 by Caroline Arnold
Photographs in this book copyright © 1988 by Arthur Arnold with
the exception of those listed on page 46.

LIBRARY OF CONGRESS CATALOGING-IN-PUBLICATION DATA

Arnold, Caroline.
  A walk on the Great Barrier Reef.

  "A Carolrhoda nature watch book."
  Includes index.
  Summary: Describes the fascinating plants and animals
which inhabit the Great Barrier Reef.
    1. Coral reef biology — Australia — Great Barrier Reef
(Qld.) — Juvenile literature. 2. Great Barrier Reef
(Qld.) — Juvenile literature. [1. Coral reef biology —
Australia. 2. Great Barrier Reef (Qld.)] I. Arnold,
Arthur, ill. II. Title.
QH197.A65   1988   574.9′1943   87-27746
ISBN 0-87614-285-4 (lib. bdg.)

Manufactured in the United States of America

1 2 3 4 5 6 7 8 9 10 98 97 96 95 94 93 92 91 90 89 88

Along the northeast coast of Australia lies a wondrous place called the Great Barrier Reef. It is an undersea wilderness filled with beautiful and fascinating plants and animals.

The Great Barrier Reef is actually a series of many smaller reefs. A **reef** forms an underwater wall. It can be made of rock, coral, or sand, and the top of it lies under or just above the surface of the sea.

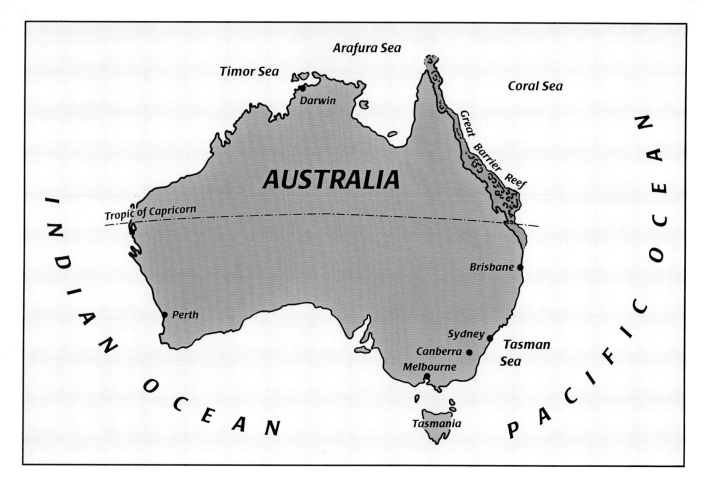

Coral reefs are found in areas of the ocean where the water is clean, warm, and not too deep. Although there are coral reefs throughout the tropical waters of the world, the Great Barrier Reef is the longest. It stretches out in a broken chain over 1,250 miles (2,000 km) and forms a natural **breakwater,** or barrier, between the pounding waves of the Pacific Ocean and the Australian coastline. The reef lies in the Coral Sea, the part of the Pacific Ocean near the northeast coast of Australia. The waters around the reef cover about 80,000 square miles (208,000 sq km)—an area slightly smaller than the state of Minnesota.

No other reef is as big or as rich with sea life as the Great Barrier Reef. Some of the most unusual and colorful forms of life on earth live on the reef itself, in the water around it, and on nearby islands. Anyone exploring the reef and its surrounding area will see multicolored fish, sea creatures both huge and tiny, reptiles, and many kinds of birds.

The polyps of this stony coral have their tentacles extended for feeding.

The most amazing fact about coral reefs is that they are formed by tiny tube-shaped animals called **coral polyps.** The body of a coral polyp is soft but has a hard outer skeleton for support and protection. **Stony coral** skeletons are the building blocks that make up the reef.

Most coral polyps measure from less than 1/16 of an inch to 5/16 of an inch (1 to 8 mm) across. Fingerlike **tentacles** surround a coral polyp's mouth. The polyp uses these tentacles to pull **zooplankton,** or tiny animals that float in bodies of water, into its mouth. The tentacles are covered with stinging cells that stun the tiny floating animals when they brush against the tentacles. Most corals feed at night and withdraw into their skeletons during the day.

In the diagram: **BUDDING** ① ② ③ ④

As the polyps bud, this coral colony will continue to grow.

The bright colors and graceful shapes of corals give them a plantlike look, but each coral growth is really a colony of tiny coral polyps. A colony grows as the polyps **bud,** or produce new polyps, which in turn produce new skeletons.

Corals form new colonies by producing **planulae.** Each tiny planula is shaped like a pear and is about 1/16 of an inch (1 mm) long. Along the outside of a planula are microscopic hairs that help it swim. Each new planula attaches itself to a hard surface and takes **calcium carbonate,** a mineral found dissolved in water, out of the seawater to grow a hard skeleton. The new polyps begin to bud, and a new coral colony grows.

Above: *Tiny, white needles of calcium carbonate are clearly visible in this graceful soft coral.*

Below: *Unlike the polyps of most stony corals, Goniopora coral polyps remain exposed during the day. If you gently brush your hand across the Goniopora polyps, they feel like plush velvet.*

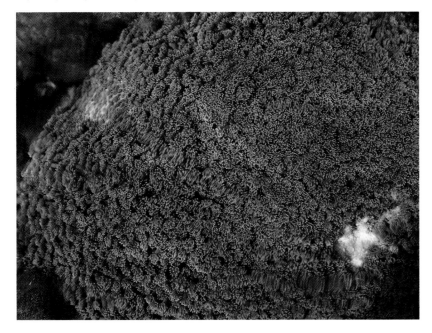

The calcium carbonate skeletons of the reef-building stony corals are extremely strong; calcium carbonate is also found in limestone, a rocklike material. Stony coral skeletons are often called limestone skeletons. Some corals have softer skeletons that contain tiny needlelike structures of calcium carbonate. These soft corals are not reef builders.

With no living polyps, this staghorn coral skeleton has lost its purplish color.

The different colors of coral come from the living tissues that are associated with the coral skeletons. These living parts include the polyps themselves and the **algae**, or tiny plants, that grow within the tissues of the polyps and in the coral skeletons. When the coral polyps and algae die, the skeleton remains. With a few exceptions, the skeleton is white.

Certain kinds of algae add more to the reef than color. **Coralline algae**, red algae, actually add to the structure of the reef by forming calcium carbonate deposits that act like cement. Pieces of dead coral are cemented together, forming the hard surfaces to which planulae attach themselves. On some parts of the reef, the stony structure of the reef wall is made up more of algae "cement" than of coral colonies. Certain kinds of green algae also contribute to the structure of the reef. When these algae die, calcium carbonate fragments in their plant tissues become part of the sand. This sand fills chinks in the reef walls making them even stronger.

Coral polyps cannot live without a constant supply of moving water to carry zooplankton to their tentacles. When coral grows up to the surface of the water, it begins to branch out sideways. The coral at the water's surface dies, and, from above, the coral formation begins to look like a submerged spiderweb. Over a long period of time, dead coral at the top of the reef collects other pieces of broken coral. Coralline algae eventually cement this coral together.

The best temperature for coral growth is between 75° and 85° Fahrenheit (24° to 29° Celsius). This is the usual water temperature along the northeast coast of Australia, so it's not surprising that the Great Barrier Reef has become so large.

Although coral will grow in water up to 250 feet deep (76 m), it grows best in shallow water. Most corals that grow below 150 feet (46 m) of water are not reef-building corals. Reef-building corals cannot live without a kind of algae that makes their home inside the bodies of coral polyps. The algae take up waste products from the polyp and convert them to nutrients that are used by the polyps. This process also speeds up the rate at which calcium carbonate is produced to form the coral skeleton.

Since the algae need sunlight to convert the waste products to nutrients, and the polyps need the algae, coral cannot grow in deep or murky water. This is why the many different kinds of reef-building corals are found in shallow waters where the sun can reach the polyps.

Coral reefs form along the shores of islands and continents. There are three different kinds of coral reef formations.

A **fringing reef** develops as coral grows in the shallow waters along the shores of an island.

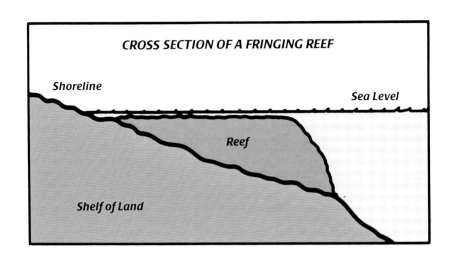

A **barrier reef**, such as the Great Barrier Reef, grows off the coast of an island or continent at some distance away from the shore. A calm **lagoon** separates the barrier reef and the shore.

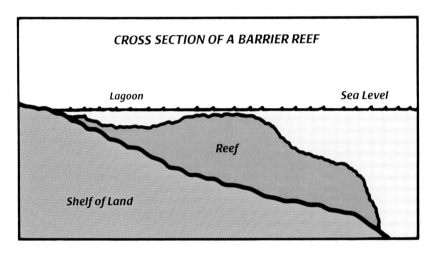

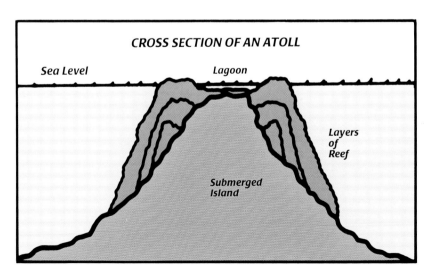

An **atoll** is a circular reef, often with a lagoon in the center. The shallow waters of the lagoon cover a submerged island.

A submerged island has created this atoll in the Palau Islands of Micronesia.

An atoll begins to form when a volcanic island with a fringing reef starts to sink because of changes that occur in the ocean floor. When this happens, the fringing reef surrounding the island sinks too. Because the reef is continually being rebuilt by new coral colonies growing on the old skeletons, it remains close to the surface of the water. With the island partially submerged, the reef becomes a barrier reef, with the new coral growths visible as an offshore barrier, and the older growths hidden by the water between the reef and the shore. Eventually the island sinks below the surface of the water, leaving only the ring of coral visible from above.

Ocean waves constantly wash over dead coral and slowly grind it to sand. This sand fills up cracks on the surface of the reef, forming the **reef flat.** Over many years, the coral sand on the reef flat gets pressed together to form a cementlike surface. This hard surface is covered by more sand. **Reef rocks,** chunks of "rock" broken from the cementlike surface, litter the reef flat. Sometimes so much sand builds up on the reef flat that a small island is formed. There are many such islands on the Great Barrier Reef. They are called **coral cays.** Most coral cays are impossible to reach by boat. The submerged reef is difficult to see, and the hard, sharp coral can easily cut a hole in the bottom of a boat. Ancient shipwrecks can still be found on many parts of the Great Barrier Reef.

Compressed coral sand forms these solid slabs of flat reef rock.

Heron Island is a coral cay on the Great Barrier Reef that has been opened up to tourists. A center for scientific research has also been established there. Helicopters land on the island, and boats approach it through a manmade channel cut into the reef.

Located on the Tropic of Capricorn, Heron Island is surrounded by a reef flat that extends nearly 1/4 mile (.4 km) into the ocean. At the seaward edge of the reef flat are huge growths of coral in about 30 feet (9 m) of water. Coral growths provide food and protection for fish and other kinds of sea life. You can see this underwater environment with snorkeling or diving gear, or through a glass-bottomed boat. No special gear, however, is needed to explore the shallow water on the reef flat at low tide.

Each day, the tide changes twice. At high tide on Heron Island, 3 to 4 feet (about 1 m) of water covers the reef flat. Then many of the larger fish leave the reef edge and swim close to shore. At low tide, as little as 3 inches (7.6 cm) of water covers the reef flat; the big fish return to deep water, the smaller fish hide in shallow pools, and the reef's surface is revealed. Then, carrying a stick for balance, and wearing canvas shoes for protection against sharp pieces of coral, you can begin to explore the reef by yourself.

18

The plants and animals that live on the underside of a reef rock need the darkness and protection the rock gives.

In the shallow waters of the reef flat, you will see pieces of gray reef rock. From above they look dull, but when you turn them over a colorful world of algae, shells, and other life appears.

Reefs like the Great Barrier Reef take thousands of years to develop. When you walk on a reef, always be careful not to step on living coral. Most grow very slowly, perhaps less than 2 inches (5 cm) a year. It can take many years to replace a broken piece.

At least 350 varieties of coral are found on the Great Barrier Reef. Each type of coral has a differently shaped outer skeleton.

Corals that look like the antlers of deer are called staghorn coral. Staghorn coral is one of the most common types of coral on the Great Barrier Reef. It is also one of the fastest-growing corals, sometimes producing as much as 4 new inches (10 cm) a year.

The round shape and grooves of the brain coral skeleton look something like a real brain. These coral polyps do not build individual limestone shelters, instead they form high, limestone walls. The polyps live in the channels created by the twisting walls. Brain coral skeletons are so strong that they have even been used as cornerstones for buildings.

Mushroom coral, unlike most corals, does not form colonies. The polyps, sometimes as large as 5 inches (12.7 cm) in diameter, form individual skeletons that resemble the underside of a mushroom.

Besides the corals, many of which make the reef itself, the Great Barrier Reef is the home of many other creatures. One of the most beautiful members of the reef community is the sea anemone.

This flowerlike animal belongs to the same **phylum**, or scientific group-

ing, as the coral polyp. Like the coral polyp, the sea anemone has a tube-shaped body topped by a tentacle-encircled mouth. Stinging cells covering the tentacles release tiny poison threads that paralyze small sea creatures and fish, which the anemone then eats.

Most sea animals learn to avoid sea anemones' painful stingers. One creature on the reef, the clownfish or anemone fish, lives among the sea anemones' tentacles. Scientists believe that this fish is protected from the poison threads by a special mucous coating on its skin. An anemone provides the clownfish with safe shelter from its enemies. The clownfish can also lay its eggs in a safe place—under the edges of the anemone. Just as the clownfish benefits from the anemone, the anemone is better off because of the clownfish. The clownfish protects the anemone from some predators and cleans the anemone. The swimming movements of the clownfish keeps sand from settling on the anemone.

Sea anemones are found in every ocean in the world. Usually they measure just a few inches across in size. On the Great Barrier Reef, however, there live giant sea anemones that can grow as big as 3 feet (almost 1 m) across!

In the shallow water of the reef flat, a bright blue sea star stands out against the white sand.

If you walk along the Great Barrier Reef, you will probably find some sea stars. These creatures belong to a phylum of animals called Echinodermata. There are more than 5,300 kinds of **echinoderms** found in oceans all over the world. Although their biology and their system of tube feet are similar, the different classes of echinoderms have completely different appearances. The star-shaped sea star looks almost nothing like the cucumber-shaped sea cucumber. Most echinoderms are either round, tube-shaped, or star-shaped.

Sea stars (often called starfish although they are not fish) are some of the most brightly colored animals on the reef.

Well named, the pincushion sea star looks like a puffy cushion.

We usually think of a sea star as having five "arms," or sections, but it may have as few as four or as many as fifty. Under each arm are rows of tiny tube feet that help the sea star move along the sea floor. Sea stars do not move quickly—they cover only 2 or 3 inches (about 5 to 8 cm) a minute.

It is difficult to destroy a sea star. If it loses an arm, the sea star simply grows a new one. This is called **regeneration**. A sea star can even grow a whole new body from one arm and part of its **central disk**.

Sea stars, though, usually reproduce by releasing millions of tiny eggs and **sperm**, or male reproductive cells, into the ocean where **fertilization** occurs. The fertilized eggs grow into **larvae**, which float in the water for about two months. Then the larvae settle to the ocean bottom and develop into tiny sea stars.

25

On the underside of the pincushion sea star you can see its mouth in the center and the tube feet lining its five arms.

The mouth of a sea star is on the underside of its body. Most sea stars eat small sea animals, such as clams or sea urchins, that are found on the ocean floor. A sea star eats in an unusual way. If the food is a shelled animal, the sea star's tube feet grip the shell. Then the sea star pushes its stomach out through its mouth and into the narrow opening between the shells. After surrounding and digesting the food, the stomach is pulled back inside the sea star's body.

One of the most dangerous creatures on the Great Barrier Reef is the crown-of-thorns sea star. Its many arms are covered with spines containing a powerful poison.

The crown-of-thorns sea star feeds on the coral polyps that make up the reef. Some parts of the Great Barrier Reef have been nearly destroyed by great numbers of crown-of-thorns. This has a drastic effect on the reef creatures, for when the coral is gone, then other life that depends on it is also destroyed.

Brittle stars got their name because their arms break off easily.

Brittle stars and serpent stars are in a **class**, or scientific grouping, of echinoderms that have thin, snakelike arms. Unlike sea stars, brittle stars and serpent stars use their arms instead of their tube feet to move quickly across the sand. These fragile animals also eat differently than sea stars. Instead of pushing their stomachs out of their mouths to surround the food, brittle stars and serpent stars use their arms to bring the food to their mouths.

The underside of this sea cucumber has a striped pattern that is different from the dull, even color of its topside.

Some of the first explorers of the Great Barrier Reef were from China. Thousands of years before Europeans went to Australia, the Chinese came looking for sea cucumbers. Sea cucumbers can be dried to make a food called trepang. Chinese merchants came to the Great Barrier Reef to collect the trepang, then returned to China to sell the dried skins.

Today at least 60 different kinds of sea cucumbers live on the Great Barrier Reef. They can be as little as an inch (2.5 cm) in length or as much as 3 feet (90 cm) long. There are many different colors of sea cucumbers.

29

A feeding sea cucumber uses tentacles to pull food into its mouth opening.

Because sea cucumbers dig into the sand and bury themselves, they are often called *bêche-de-mer* (besh-duh-mair), a French word meaning "spade of the sea." A sea cucumber feeds on tiny animals and plants in the water and in the sand. It uses tentacles that surround its head end to pull the food into its mouth. Waste, including the sand that it has taken in, is pushed out the other end. Although a few sea cucumbers protect themselves with poison, most are harmless.

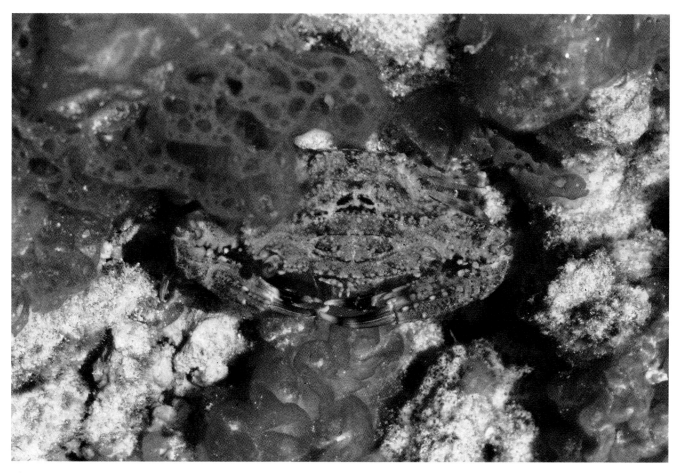

Although this blue crab was found on the reef flat that surrounds Heron Island, blue crabs can also be found in the colder waters along North America's eastern coast.

Many kinds of crabs live on the Great Barrier Reef. In the water and sometimes on the land, you can see tiny hermit crabs that carry their seashell homes with them. The shell protects the hermit crab's exposed abdomen. Pale ghost crabs, on the other hand, do not carry their homes with them but burrow in the sand beaches adjacent to the reef flat.

Crabs belong to a class of animals called Crustacea. Like all **crustaceans,** the crab has no bones. Their soft bodies are divided into many segments that are protected by a hard outer shell. The shell is made of a substance called **chitin** (kie-ton) and is like a suit of armor for the crab. As the crab grows, it sheds the shell that has become too small and develops a new one. The crab's strong claws are used both for protection and for catching other reef animals for food.

It may be hard to think of worms as beautiful creatures. Yet the worms on the Great Barrier Reef are brightly colored and have unusual shapes. Some can be found hiding under reef rocks in shallow water. Others swim in deeper water.

Flatworms are among the most color-ful reef worms. People call them magic carpet worms because those that swim in deep water look like multihued flying carpets as they glide through the water. Most flatworms are creeping forms that live in crevices and under rocks and vary in size from under an inch to about 4 inches (about .1 cm to 10 cm).

The tentacles on some tubeworms have a featherlike appearance. These tubeworms are commonly called featherduster worms or Christmas tree worms.

Tubeworms live on the reef flats as well as in deeper water. These worms stay in one place, living in tubes that they form themselves or burrowing inside coral skeletons. When the worms that live in coral pop their colorful heads out to feed, people often mistake them for living coral polyps.

These cowries, found clinging to the underside of a reef rock, are about 3/4 of an inch (2 cm) long.

Although they look very different from each other, the octopus, the sea hare, and the clam are all members of the same phylum, Mollusca. They all have unsegmented bodies with no inner skeleton. **Mollusks'** soft bodies are often enclosed in hard shells. There are over 100,000 different kinds of mollusks, and many of them live on the Great Barrier Reef.

Cowrie shells and cone shells are **gastropods,** or mollusks that are members of the class Gastropoda. These and other one-shelled marine snails are also called **univalves.** Cowrie shells and cone shells are just two of the many univalves that can be found on the reef flat, either attached to reef rocks or creeping across the sand.

Cowries have a beautifully polished shell because this snail is able to extend its **mantle,** tissue that covers part of every snail's body, to cover its shell. The covered shell is protected from scratches and from tiny plants and animals that might otherwise find a home on the surface of the shell.

This cone shell measures about 3 inches (7.6 cm) long.

Most mollusks with shells hide in them when danger is near, but the cone shell snail comes outside its shell to defend itself. Each cone shell snail has a long tube filled with poisonous barbs. The sharp tip of the barb injects the poison into an attacker, so the cone shell is also called arrow tongue. Normally the poisonous barbs are used to capture the sea worms and fish that are often the cone shell's food.

A sea hare can grow to be up to a foot (30 cm) long.

Some mollusks, such as the sea slug and the octopus, do not have any shells. Others, such as the sea hare, have small shells hidden inside their bodies. Without hard outer shells, these animals protect themselves in other ways. Some swim fast; others have protective coloring.

The sea hare is difficult to spot on the reef because it is the same color as the sand, coral, and algae. Also, when it is disturbed, the sea hare shoots out an inky cloud so enemies cannot see it. In ancient times, the Roman scientist Pliny thought that this strange animal looked something like a crouching rabbit, so he named it the sea hare.

The reef clam is one of the biggest and most common of the shelled mollusks found on the reef flat. Clams are called **bivalves** and belong to the class Bivalvia. Bivalves have two shells held together by hinges.

The crusty shells of the reef clam are about 12 inches (30 cm) long. You will often find the reef clam wedged among the corals on the reef flat. Its shells will be partly open to let water flow through. Like so many other reef creatures, the clam eats zooplankton, the tiny animals that float in the water. When touched, the clam will use strong muscles to close its shells.

A huge grouper is the subject of this diver's picture. The grouper is a sharp-toothed fish that eats other fish but is not dangerous to people.

Many of the most colorful and interesting fish in the world live in the waters of the Great Barrier Reef. People come from all over the world to see huge groupers, colorful clownfish, striped zebra fish, sharks, and many other kinds of fish.

The slow-moving box fish is found in shallow water. Its square shape and bright coloring make it easy to see.

To see most of these fish, you must dive in deep water or snorkel on the reef flat at high tide. Although many fish remain on the reef flat at low tide, they hide or swim away when people come near. If you peer into shallow pools on the reef flat, though, you may see some fish darting among the coral.

Birds and people are the main daytime visitors to the sandy beaches of the coral cays. If you walk the beach on a warm summer night, though, you might be lucky enough to see another creature of the reef—the green sea turtle. Unable to withstand cold temperatures, green sea turtles thrive in the warm waters around the Great Barrier Reef.

When fully grown, a green sea turtle may weigh as much as 300 pounds (136 kg) and have a shell 4 feet (1.2 m) long.

The nesting season for green turtles is between October and March, summertime on the Great Barrier Reef. At night, a female turtle leaves the water and slowly crawls up onto the sand. The female returns year after year to the same island. At the top of the beach, she uses both her front and rear flippers to form a shallow dish. Then, with her rear flippers, she digs a deep hole within the shallow dish and lays about 100 eggs in the hole. Each egg has a white rubbery shell and is about the size of a golf ball. After covering the eggs with sand, the turtle goes back to the water.

When the eggs hatch 10 weeks later, the young turtles crawl out of the nest and make their way into the water. The tiny, newly hatched turtles are easy prey for birds, ghost crabs, and other predators, and many do not make it to the sea. Those that do will live their whole lives in the water. The males will never again go ashore, and the females only come back to the shore to lay eggs.

Female loggerhead and hawksbill turtles also lay their eggs on the reef flats of the Great Barrier Reef. Turtles are **reptiles.** Although many reptiles live in water, they cannot breathe in water as fish do. Sea turtles can stay underwater for 20 or 30 minutes at a time. Then they must come to the surface of the water to breathe air.

Another reptile found in Great Barrier Reef waters is the sea snake. Sea snakes have flat tails that they use as paddles for swimming. Sea snakes are poisonous, but their fangs are so small that they cannot inject much poison in one bite. It is unusual to see sea snakes on the reef flat.

Heron Island got its name from the reef herons that live there. This white heron has built a large nest of sticks on the top of the tree.

Each year, millions of birds come to the small coral islands of the Great Barrier Reef. Some birds travel up to 12,500 miles (20,000 km) to get there! They are attracted by the fish and sea animals that live on and around the reef. These provide food for both migrating and nesting birds.

Heron Island and a few other coral cays on the Great Barrier Reef are covered with trees. Birds are partly responsible for this tree cover.

When first formed, a coral cay island is just a mound of sand on top of the coral. Sea birds rest on it, dropping seeds of plants they have picked up in other places. Seeds may also be carried to an island by the wind or washed to shore by waves. Soil may be blown from land nearby onto a newly formed island and some of the seeds will begin to grow.

The white-capped noddy tern likes to build its nest in the pinsonia trees of Heron Island. Each pair of noddies claims one branch where they build their nest with seaweed and leaves.

The trees on Heron Island provide protection from the weather and predators. They are also good nesting places.

So many noddies sharing a single tree create a sort of noddy tern apartment house.

The variety of life on the reef is so rich that each walk on it or along its island shores reveals new animals and plants. The Great Barrier Reef and the many forms of life that depend on it are one of the natural wonders of the world. Yet, like many other natural areas into which humans have intruded, this reef is in danger. When humans disturb the delicate balance of life on the reef, the reef itself is damaged.

On October 21, 1979, the Australian government made the part of the reef that includes Heron Island into a national park. This will help insure the preservation of wildlife on this part of the Great Barrier Reef so that people in the future will be able to visit the reef and explore its wonders for themselves.

GLOSSARY

algae: tiny plants that usually live in the water. The singular form of the word is alga.

atoll: a circular coral reef with a lagoon in the center

barrier reef: a coral reef that lies parallel to the shore and is separated from the shore by a lagoon

bivalve: a mollusk with a shell that is composed of two movable parts

breakwater: an offshore structure, such as a wall, that protects a harbor or beach from the force of waves

budding: when an organism forms an outgrowth that develops into a new individual

calcium carbonate: a mineral that is found in many natural substances including coral skeletons, limestone, bones, and shells

central disk: the central body part of a sea star containing the internal organs

chitin: a horny substance that forms part of the hard outer layer of some insects and crustaceans

class: the third level of seven scientific groupings that classify animals and plants according to the similarity of their biology. The members of the first grouping are less alike than the members of the seventh grouping, which are very similar.

coral cay: a low island or reef made of coral and sand

coral polyp: a tiny, soft-bodied animal that produces either a soft or a hard outer skeleton

coralline algae: a calcium-carbonate-producing red algae

crustacean: an animal belonging to the class Crustacea. Crustaceans have no bones but have an outer skeleton covering a segmented body.

echinoderm: an animal belonging to the phylum Echinodermata. Animals in this phylum have a similar internal skeleton and biology and usually have a warty or spiny outer covering.

fertilization: when a sperm and an egg unite so that an embryo may develop

fringing reef: a coral reef that forms in shallow waters along the shores of an island or continent

gastropod: an animal belonging to the class Gastropoda. Gastropods have a univalve shell or no shell.

lagoon: a calm, shallow body of water that often shares water with a larger body of water

larva: an early form of an animal, recently hatched from an egg, that must go through a stage or stages of change before it reaches its adult form. The plural form of the word is larvae.

mantle: a tissue of living cells that lines the shell opening of shell-bearing mollusks and produces shell material

mollusk: an animal belonging to the phylum Mollusca. Animals in this phylum have a soft, unsegmented body with no inner skeleton.

phylum: the second level of seven scientific groupings that classify animals and plants according to the similarity of their biology. The members of the first grouping are less alike than the members of the seventh grouping, which are very similar.

planulae: very young, free-swimming organisms that do not yet resemble the parent organism. The singular form of the word is planula.

reef: an underwater wall made of rock, coral, or sand with a top that reaches the surface of the water

reef flat: an area on the surface of the reef that is formed by the gradual buildup of coral sand

reef rock: a chunk broken from cementlike pressed coral sand

regeneration: the regrowth of an injured body part or the growth of a new body from a body part

reptile: a cold-blooded animal that has dry, scaly skin and breathes with lungs

sperm: male reproductive cell

stony coral: coral polyps that produce skeletons of calcium carbonate that are the building blocks of the reef

tentacle: an elongated and flexible projection that usually extends from around an animal's mouth. The tentacles of both anemones and polyps are covered with stinging cells.

univalve: a mollusk with a one-piece shell

zooplankton: tiny animals that live, floating or weakly swimming, in a body of water

INDEX

algae, 10-11, 12, 13, 19
anemone fish. *See* clownfish
atoll, 14; formation of, 15

birds, 6, 39, 42-43
brittle star, 28
budding, 8

calcium carbonate, 8-9, 11, 13
clam, 26, 34, 37
clownfish, 23, 38
cone shell. *See* snails
coral. *See* coral polyp
coral cays, 16-17, 39, 42
coral polyp: description of, 7; eating
    habits of, 7, 12; growth of, 8, 12-13,
    19; types of, 20-21
coral reef, 6; composition of, 7, 9, 11,
    12; destruction of, 27, 44; types of,
    14-15
coral skeleton, 7-10, 13, 20, 21, 33
cowrie shell. *See* snails
crab, 31, 40
crown-of-thorns sea star. *See* sea stars
crustaceans, 31

echinoderms, 24-30

fish, 6, 18, 23, 38-39; as food, 22, 35

gastropods, 34-36

Heron Island, 17-18, 42-43, 44

mollusks, 34-37

octopus, 34, 36

planulae, 8, 11

reef, 5. *See also* coral reef
reef-building coral. *See* stony coral
reptiles, 6, 39-41

sea anemone, 22-23
sea cucumber, 24, 29-30
sea hare, 34, 36
sea slug, 36
sea snake, 41
sea stars, 24-27, 28
serpent star, 28
snails, 34-35
soft coral, 9
starfish. *See* sea stars
stony coral, 7, 9, 13

tentacles, 7, 22, 30, 33
turtles, 39-41

worms, 32-33, 35

zooplankton, 7, 12, 37

ABOUT THE
AUTHOR AND PHOTOGRAPHER

Caroline Arnold is the author of numerous widely acclaimed books for young readers including the Carolrhoda Nature Watch title *Saving the Peregrine Falcon*, an ALA Notable Book. Ms. Arnold is also an instructor in the UCLA extension writers' program. Her husband and collaborator, **Arthur Arnold**, is a neurobiologist at UCLA. He became interested in photography as a high school student and now takes photographs for his own scientific research and as a hobby. The Arnolds live in Los Angeles with their two children.